EUGÈNE BOUDIN

E. Boudin

by JEAN SELZ

CROWN PUBLISHERS, INC. - NEW YORK

Title page: EUGÈNE BOUDIN PAINTING IN HIS STUDIO
Photograph

Translated from the French by:
SHIRLEY JENNINGS

Collection published under the direction of:
MADELEINE LEDIVELEC-GLOECKNER

Library of Congress Cataloging in Publication Data
Selz, Jean.
  Boudin.

  1. Boudin, Eugène, 1824–1898.   2. Landscape painters
–France–Biography.   I. Title.
ND553.B73S44   1982   759.4 [B]   81–19603
ISBN 0–517–547104   AACR2

PRINTED IN ITALY – INDUSTRIE GRAFICHE CATTANEO S.P.A., BERGAMO – © 1982 BONFINI PRESS CORPORATION, NAEFELS, SWITZERLAND
ALL RIGHTS IN THE U.S.A. ARE RESERVED BY CROWN PUBLISHERS, INC., NEW YORK, NEW YORK

SAILBOATS, 1862–65. Pastel, 5⁷⁄₈″ × 8″ (15 × 20.3 cm)
Gallery Marwan Hoss, Paris

In memory of Monique Jourdan-Frédérix

Perhaps it is due to the small size of its harbor that Honfleur has escaped the ravages of time, the devastation and rebuilding which, in the aftermath of war, have disfigured the majority of large European seaports. Passing in front of the monumental door of the harbor master's office, surmounted by a Virgin and Child between two slate-capped turrets, or walking around the docks, along the Sainte-Catherine wharf with its narrow gray or brown houses, or down the Saint-Etienne wharf where the former chapel today houses the Vieux Honfleur Museum, the traveler is struck by the contrast between the age-old stones and the ever-changing sky, with clouds constantly scudding before the Seine estuary wind. It is this breath of the past mingling with the fresh sea breezes that seems to whisper in the ear a name that still haunts the entire Normandy coast: Eugène Boudin.

STROLLING ON THE BEACH, 1863
Oil on wood, 10¼" × 15¾" (26 × 40 cm)
Private collection

HONFLEUR, LOW TIDE, 1856
Oil on wood, $10^{7}/_{8}'' \times 15^{3}/_{4}''$ (27.5 × 40 cm)
Private collection

Sitting Woman and Child, before 1855
Conté crayon, 5¹/₈″ × 3³/₄″ (13 × 9.2 cm)
Private collection

FARM NEAR QUIMPER, 1858. Oil on wood, 15″ × 22″ (38 × 56 cm)
Private collection

25 Janvier 1852

10

Portrait of a Woman, 1852
Pencil, 6¹³/₁₆″ × 4¹/₂″ (17.3 × 11.3 cm)
Louvre, Cabinet des Dessins, Paris

STILL LIFE WITH LOBSTER
ON A WHITE TABLECLOTH, 1853–1856
Oil on canvas, 22¹/₂″ × 32¹/₄″ (58 × 82 cm)
The High Museum of Art, Atlanta, Georgia.
Gift in memory of Lena B. Jacobs

The Pilgrimage at Sainte-Anne-La-Palud, 1858. Oil on canvas, 30¹¹/₁₆″ × 61″ (78 × 155 cm)
Musée des Beaux-Arts André Malraux, Le Havre, France

One day when I was bathing on the beach at Deauville, I could not help seeing that I was almost the only person in the water, although there were plenty of people sitting or lying near the beach huts: things had changed little since the time when Boudin was painting his famous *Beach Scenes*, where the beauties of the Second Empire strolled beneath their parasols, but no one was ever shown actually in the sea. Of course, the background had changed, and Boudin would not have seen the luxurious villas, the big hotels, and the modern casino.

Deauville and Trouville were fashionable French seaside resorts in the nineteenth century. How could Boudin, deliberately shunning all frivolous pleasures, have spent so much of his life on those beaches, returning almost every summer, even after he had known Brittany, the South of France and Venice? It is a question that the story of his life will unfold.

Honfleur . . . Deauville — only about ten miles separate the two towns. Yet between them stretched Eugène Boudin's entire life, born at Honfleur in 1824, died at Deauville in 1898.

CABIN BOY AT HONFLEUR, STATIONER AT LE HAVRE

The prelude to Boudin's life was the sea, which would later provide the subject of so much of his work. His father, Léonard-Sébastien Boudin (1789–1863), was a seaman, who came from a long line of Honfleur sailors. At the age of eleven Léonard went to sea as a cabin boy on a fireship where he served his apprenticeship for the navy. In 1811, as a gunner on board the frigate « L'Amazone, » he took part in a naval battle against the English. Subsequently he became a member of the crew of a schooner fishing for cod off the coast of Newfoundland. In 1816 he married Marie-Félicité Buffet, and Louis-Eugène Boudin was born eight years later, on July 12, 1824. The house where he was born can still be seen at Honfleur in Rue Bourdet.

After spending a number of years on a Honfleur fishing boat, Léonard Boudin assumed command of a trader plying between Honfleur and Rouen. It was on this small boat nicknamed « Le Polichinelle » that the young Eugène, following in his father's footsteps at about the same age, began to work as a cabin boy. And it was during his spare time when sailing up and down the river that Eugène made his first sketches.

In 1835 Léonard Boudin was employed by the Albrecht Shipping Company, whose boats sailed between Le Havre and Hamburg. The family moved to Le Havre, and Eugène spent a year at a school run by priests. Here he developed his taste for drawing and received a prize for calligraphy. In the Boudin family, however, no one was expected to stay at school for long, and at the age of twelve Eugène went to work as a clerk, first with a Le Havre publisher and printer, Joseph Morlent, in Place de la Comédie, and afterward in a stationer's shop in Rue des Drapiers where he was soon promoted to secretary to the owner, Alphonse Lemasle. Boudin worked in the shop until 1842. Humble as it was, the job was not without consequences for the painter's future, as it was Lemasle who gave him his first paintbox.

About this time steamship navigation was developing in France, encouraged by the first crossing of the Atlantic in 1819 by the steamer « Le Savannah. » In 1838 the small steamer « Le Français » began to ply between Le Havre and Honfleur, and Léonard Boudin

The Beach at Trouville, 1864. Oil on wood, 10¼″ × 18½″ (26.4 × 47.5 cm)
Collection: Mr. and Mrs. Paul Mellon

THE BEACH AT TROUVILLE, 1863. Oil on canvas, $13^{5}/_{8}'' \times 22^{3}/_{8}''$ (35×57 cm)
Collection: Mr. and Mrs. Paul Mellon

The Artist's Father,
Léonard-Sébastien Boudin, c. 1858–60
Pencil, 8 1/2″ × 5 1/2″ (21.5 × 14 cm)
Private collection

BEACH SCENE, 1863
Watercolor and pastel,
7 1/2″ × 11 13/16″ (19 × 30 cm)
Musée Marmottan, Paris

ON THE BEACH AT TROUVILLE, 1863
Oil on wood, 10″ × 18″ (25.4 × 45.7 cm)
The Metropolitan Museum of Art, New York.
Bequest of Amelia B. Lazarus

THE JETTY AT TROUVILLE: SUNSET, 1862
Oil on wood, 10¼″ × 18⅞″ (26 × 48 cm)
Ashmoleum Museum, Oxford

CONCERT AT THE CASINO OF DEAUVILLE, 1865. Oil on canvas, $16^{3}/_{8}$" × 29" (41.5 × 73.5 cm)
Collection: Mr. and Mrs. Paul Mellon

served on it as a seaman for the next twenty-four years. At the same time his wife worked as a stewardess on a number of Le Havre ships, including the «Normandie» which in 1840 carried Napoleon's coffin from Cherbourg, where it had been brought by «La Belle Poule,» to Val-de-la-Haye near Rouen. In spite of his experience as a cabin boy on board his father's «Le Polichinelle,» Eugène was not tempted to become a sailor. In 1844 he decided to go into partnership with Jean Acher, one of Lemasle's foremen, in order to set up a stationer's shop at 18 rue de la Communauté.

What interested Boudin was not so much the stationery business but the fact that he and his partner also framed pictures, so that there were always one or two paintings by visiting artists on display in the shop. Boudin, who was just beginning to try his hand at painting, welcomed the opportunity of being able to examine firsthand the work of artists some ten to twenty years older than he, and even get to know the painters personally. His new friends included Thomas Couture, Constant Troyon, and Eugène Isabey (the son of Jean-Baptiste Isabey, the Empire portrait painter). Jean-François Millet also used to visit Le Havre and spent several months there in 1845. At the time he was mainly interested in portraits and had not yet taken to landscape painting. Nevertheless, it was Millet who corrected the first landscape attempted by Boudin under the influence of Troyon. Millet was full of good advice, but as soon as he realized that the young picture framer was determined to become a painter, he felt obliged to warn him of the countless difficulties that beset an artist's life.

Millet was quite right. The next year the two partners quarreled and Boudin left the stationer's shop to devote his time to drawing and studying watercolor. Life at the time was far from easy.

A PROVINCIAL IN PARIS

Always busy with his pencils and paintbox, Boudin spent his days at the harbor or on the neighboring coast where he fell under the spell of the shore and the sea and the cloud-filled skies. It was a love he never lost. And we learn from his notebooks that it was only his passion for painting that comforted him in the gloominess of his everyday life.

Boudin lived with his family at 51 Grand-Quai, above a restaurant where the owner, Audièvre, introduced him to one of his customers, Théodule Ribot, with whom Boudin became great friends. Later still on the Grand-Quai, he set up a small studio on the fourth floor where, when he was not working at the harbor or in the old part of the town, he would paint bunches of flowers and still lifes. By the end of the year Boudin was able to find one or two patrons who bought his pictures for the modest sum of ten francs apiece, a slight income that nevertheless made all the difference to the aspiring artist.

Encouraged by this first success but only too well aware of how little Le Havre could offer in the way of artistic education, Boudin longed to go to Paris to see the painters he had already met and be able to visit the museums and study the old masters. It was a dream he was able to realize in 1847 when he arrived in the capital with his hard-earned savings. In spite of all the bustle and animation of the big city, life was not very exciting for a lonely young man from the provinces. Boudin spent whole days in the Louvre, learning a great deal from the famous paintings, but realizing at the same time what a huge gap separated his own work from the achievements of the masters. Indeed, as we learn from

Beach Scene, 1865
Pencil and watercolor, 4¹⁵/₁₆″ × 7¹/₁₆″ (12.5 × 18 cm)
Private collection

his letters and notebooks, Boudin was always a harsh judge of his pictures and even at the height of his powers would despair of ever being able to express himself fully in his painting.

In love with the landscape of France, he was never very enthusiastic about going abroad. The first time he did so was at the instigation of Baron Taylor to whom he had been recommended. The Baron was an eccentric character with a finger in many pies. He had abandoned a military career probably because he felt it was incompatible with his interest in art and literature. Baron Taylor was, successively, senator under the Empire, playwright, royal commissioner to the Comédie-Française, head of several archaeological expeditions (he was instrumental in bringing the Luxor obelisk back to France), independent member of the Académie des Beaux-Arts, and inspector general of the Beaux-Arts. But he is above all remembered as a benefactor who organized mutual aid societies to provide help for struggling writers and artists. In this connection the Baron entrusted Boudin with a publicity tour in the north of France and Belgium. Boudin was accompanied by the sculptor Rochet, the now forgotten author of statues of Charlemagne and Bonaparte. Their task was to sell charity lottery tickets for the benefit of poor artists and writers.

Boudin visited Arras, Lille, Valenciennes, and Saint-Amand before going on to Belgium where he found time to study the Flemish masters in the museums. That was in 1849, and twenty years later he would return to paint the canals, the ports, and the banks of the Scheldt—his favorite subjects seen beneath a different sky.

Boudin's earliest known works are dated 1850: *The Return of the Gleaners* and *The Return of the Hunters*. But like all young painters of his time he made innumerable copies of old masters, some of which have survived. Boudin even made some money from his copies. For example, Baron Taylor commissioned a copy of *Traveler's Rest* by Adriaen Van Ostade and copies of works by Watteau, Lancret, and Joseph Vernet. Boudin was particularly fond of the Dutch landscape painters and above all the artists who painted seascapes. Yet, however closely he studied the way in which the Van de Veldes represented the sails and rigging, it took some years before he succeeded in painting ships to his own satisfaction.

Boudin returned to Le Havre, where in 1850, a Société des Amis des Arts had organized a small biennial exhibition of painting at which the artist for the first time showed a number of his pictures. Two of them were bought by the Society's Purchases Committee, and the organizers, interested in the work of the young painter, petitioned the municipality to make him an annual grant of 1,200 francs for a period of three years, to enable him to go to Paris to continue his studies. Thomas Couture and Constant Troyon were enthusiastic in their support of the request. Boudin was awarded the grant in February 1851, «on condition,» stated the municipality, «that he send to Le Havre every year one or two pictures for the museum, if they are considered good enough.»

Boudin returned to Paris on June 30, 1851. But it is hardly surprising that anyone used to being out in the fresh air beside his favorite subject, the sea, should have found it difficult to remain shut up in Paris for three years. Not much information is available on the way he spent his time, but we do know that he often escaped from the city to stay in his beloved Normandy. Boudin did not appear to be in any hurry to send specimens of his work to Le Havre. In 1852, however, he showed eleven pictures at an exhibition in Le Havre Museum and was able to sell two of them. Little is known about the paintings he delivered in return for his grant, except for one or two still lifes and two copies, one of *The Meadow* by Paul Potter and the other of *The Stream* by Ruysdaël (today in Le Havre Museum). Altogether the Le Havre municipality does not seem to have been very pleased

Beach Scene, 1867
Ink and watercolor
Ashmoleum Museum, Oxford

BATHING TIME AT DEAUVILLE, 1865
Oil on wood, 13⅝" × 22¾" (34 × 57 cm)
Collection: Mr. and Mrs Paul Mellon

25

On the Beach at Sunset, 1865.   Oil on wood, 14¹⁄₈″ × 22³⁄₈″ (36 × 57 cm)
Collection: Mr. Walter H. Annenberg

THE BEACH AT VILLERVILLE, 1864. Oil on canvas, 17¾″ × 29½″ (45 × 75 cm)
National Gallery of Art, Washington, D.C. Chester Dale Collection

THE BEACH AT TROUVILLE, 1864
Oil on wood, 10¼″ × 18⅞″ (26 × 48 cm)
Louvre, Musée du Jeu de Paume, Paris

APPROACHING STORM, 1864. Oil on panel, $14\frac{3}{8}'' \times 22\frac{3}{4}''$ (36.5 × 58 cm)
The Art Institute of Chicago.
Gift of Annie Swan Coburn to the Coburn Memorial Collection

THE BEACH AT TROUVILLE, 1865
Pastel, 7¼″ × 10¾″ (18.5 × 27.5 cm)
Private collection

On the Beach at Trouville, 1865
Oil on wood, 7¼″ × 10¾″ (18.3 × 27.3 cm)
Private collection

31

BEACH SCENE AT TROUVILLE, 1869. Oil on wood, 13³⁄₄″ × 22¹⁄₂″ (34.5 × 57 cm)
Private collection

either with its protégé or with the way his painting was developing. In fact, Boudin, although sometimes inspired by well-known landscape artists like Corot, Rousseau, and Troyon, was steadily pursuing that personal vision that would lead him to the verge of Impressionism. It was not a course that was likely to be appreciated by the proponents of « good painting » — the kind of painting that received medals at the Salon. Whatever the reason, once the three years were up, Boudin's grant was not renewed.

FIRST SEASCAPES

In 1854 Boudin was back in Le Havre where he lived first in Rue de l'Orangerie and later in Rue Séry. His « Notebooks » contain reflections on his work and his own feelings, revealing something of his persistence in the face of uncertainty and disappointment. On March 25, 1854, he wrote: « Nature is far richer than I can represent her. » And later: « Sometimes when I am walking in a melancholy mood, I look at the light which bathes the earth, shimmers on the water and plays on people's clothing and I feel positively faint at the idea of how much genius is necessary to overcome so many difficulties. » On April 6 he wrote: « What is missing from my painting? Almost nothing and everything. The effect is not right. There is too little color. ... My brush strokes are awkward, my colors are insipid: my execution lacks verve, I shall have to start all over again. »

It would be interesting to compare Boudin's pessimism with the work he was actually doing at the time, but few of his paintings have survived from the early fifties. There is a portrait of his father *Léonard-Sébastien Boudin* in Le Havre Museum; Boudin was not, however, a good portrait painter. There are also one or two still lifes including *Still Life with Lobster on a white Tablecloth,** and a number of studies of trees, but three are still very few seascapes or harbors. This may well be due to the difficulty Boudin found in reconciling the precision required for drawing a ship's complicated rigging with the kind of fluidity and liveliness of style he was constantly striving to achieve. The result was that in about 1852 Boudin began to work in collaboration with Cassinelli, a painter who was good at drawing masts. The two artists jointly signed a number of pictures where it is easy to see the difference between the meticulous way the ships are painted and the style Boudin himself would develop a few years later. At the time, however, before Boudin had made a name for himself, it seems that pictures signed Boudin and Cassinelli sold better than canvases painted by Boudin alone.

On July 18, 1854, Boudin moved to Honfleur where he spent three months with Madame Toutain at the Saint-Siméon farm, a favorite rendezvous for painters. A great many painters have stayed there including — to confine ourselves to the nineteenth century — Français, Diaz, Harpignies, Dubourg, Troyon, and Jongkind (later the farm would lose its rusticity to become a proper hotel, as it still is today). In 1859 Courbet painted *Madame Toutain's Garden.* Earlier, Eugene Isabey had been coming to Honfleur since 1827 (he painted a *Beach at Honfleur*) and was soon followed by Paul Huet and Corot, who painted the beautiful *Honfleur, Houses on the Quays* around 1830. To the end of his life Boudin frequently returned to Honfleur where he painted a large number of pictures: *Notre-Dame*

---

* See page 11.

34

Fishermen and Boat, undated
Pencil, 3 15/16″ × 5 3/4″ (10 × 14.5 cm)
Private collection
◁

◁
Sitting Figures on the Shore
and Boat, undated
Pencil
Private collection

Figures and Boat, Low Tide,
before 1858
Pencil, 4 1/8″ × 8 1/4″ (10.5 × 21 cm)
Private collection

Beach Scene at Trouville, c. 1865–66
Lead Pencil, 7$^1/_{16}$″ × 10$^5/_8$″ (18 × 27 cm)
Private collection

BEACH SCENE, 1865–66
Watercolor, 6³/₄″ × 9⁷/₈″ (17 × 25 cm)
Private collection

BEACH SCENE AT TROUVILLE, 1867. Oil on wood, $7\frac{7}{8}'' \times 13\frac{3}{4}''$ (20 × 35 cm)
Private collection

THE BEACH AT TROUVILLE, 1867. Oil on canvas, 24³/₄″ × 35″ (63.5 × 90.4 cm)
Private collection

BEACH SCENE, 1865. Watercolor, $6^{3}/_{8}'' \times 10^{1}/_{2}''$ (16.3 × 26.5 cm)
Private collection

da Grâce, The Harbor, American Three-Master Putting Out to Sea, Drinkers at Saint-Siméon, Fisherman Mending his Nets, Honfleur, Low Tide, * *The July 14ᵗʰ Regattas,* ** *The Pier at Honfleur*, etc. But in 1854 when he returned to Le Havre at the end of October, Boudin wrote: « I have come back discouraged. ... I am penniless, without the slightest means of subsistence. ... I am disgusted with everything I do. » On December 12 he was a little more hopeful: « Nevertheless I have a feeling I shall succeed, but it is a slow process and I am already thirty: besides I live in a stupid environment. »

Was it in order to escape from the « stupid environment » that the next year he went to a neighboring but totally different seaside? He spent the summer in Brittany where he seems to have found the Atlantic at first sight somewhat disconcerting. At Douarnenez he painted seascapes (*Fishing Boats at the Quay*) and in the region of Quimper he turned to landscapes. He also sketched the Breton women in the markets, fascinated by their costume and gestures.

The notebooks of February 1856 show Boudin encouraged by one or two commissions he had received. But this did not last long. In November he wrote: « I am sad and lonely. I never have a peaceful day. ... I bought some fruit and vegetables to paint — with my last two francs. »

This did not prevent him from dreaming about what would be the most enchanting aspect of his work: « To steep oneself in the sky. To capture the tenderness of the clouds. To let the cloud masses float in the background, far off in the gray mist, and then make the blue blaze forth. »

Boudin was back in Brittany in 1857, writing to his brother Louis on July 12: « I am in good health, traveling all over Finistère without being able to find anywhere that satisfies me. » And, speaking of Brest: « The harbor is beautiful, no doubt, but apart from that it is not up to our own coast. » Two days later, however, he was full of enthusiasm for the pilgrimage of Sainte-Anne-La-Palud of which he made a great many sketches that he would use for the composition of a large picture. Meanwhile, thanks to one of his friends, a number of Boudin's paintings where exhibited in Paris at the Concert Musard, Rue Basse-du-Rampart (which would later become part of the Boulevard de la Madeleine). Two of Boudin's pictures were bought by Alexandre Dumas Fils.

A number of works painted by Boudin in Brittany, or composed from sketches he brought back with him, were among the eleven paintings he exhibited in 1858 at Le Havre Société des Amis des Arts. Judging by the *Farm near Quimper,* *** dated the same year, it would seem that the painter, although not yet the accomplished colorist he would become a little later, was already the equal of Corot in the subtlety of his browns and blues and in rendering the quality of the light, and that, like Corot, he possessed the gift of evoking the dreamy poetical beauty of a landscape.

CLAUDE MONET AND CHARLES BAUDELAIRE

About this time a young man of eighteen, the son of a grocer who had set up shop in Le Havre twelve years before, was beginning to make a small reputation in the town by drawing caricatures. His name was Oscar-Claude Monet (Oscar would later disappear

---

* See page 7.   ** See back cover.   *** See page 9.

Beach Scene, 1864
Pencil and watercolor, 5$^{1}/_{2}$" × 8$^{5}/_{8}$" (14 × 22 cm)
Private collection

from his signature). Boudin had noted his skillful drawing and the humor of his unkind character sketches. For his part the young Monet had seen Boudin's paintings and did not like them at all. When the two men met, the painter complimented the caricaturist and begged him not to rest on his laurels but to turn toward the study of nature and learn to see and paint landscapes. But Monet was not interested. Gradually, however, he let himself be persuaded and bought himself a paintbox one day. Boudin took Monet with him when he was working outside and began to show him the secrets of landscape painting. Monet, who became increasingly fond of Boudin and always remained grateful to him, would say later: «My eyes, at last, were opened» and «If I have become a painter, it is entirely due to Eugène Boudin.»

Very different was Boudin's meeting with Courbet in June 1859. Courbet was forty years old and already a famous artist who had painted *Burial at Ornans* (1855) and *Young Women on the Banks of the Seine* (1857). It was he who, having admired Boudin's seascapes at a dealer in Le Havre, wanted to make his acquaintance. The two painters became friends at once and Boudin took Courbet off to Honfleur where he stayed at the Saint-Siméon farm.

It was thanks to Courbet, with whom he was out walking, that Boudin met Baudelaire down by the Honfleur harbor. The poet, who was a friend of Courbet, was staying with his mother, Madame Aupick. Since the death of her second husband, General Aupick, in 1857, she had retired to her «Toy House» at Honfleur where she would live until her death in 1871.

Boudin was fortunate that Baudelaire had seen his paintings and «several hundred pastel studies of the sea and sky» that he would remember when writing his article on the «Salon of 1859» in the «Revue française.» For it was the first year that Boudin sent a large picture to the Salon des Artistes français, *The Pilgrimage at Sainte-Anne-La-Palud* * (bought by the city of Le Havre in 1860 for 500 francs). Baudelaire described it as «a very good and painstaking picture.» Painstaking is the right word because the painting, which includes over sixty figures, is somewhat laboriously composed in a rather stilted style. Clearly the artist had not succeeded in expressing himself as freely as in his studies of the sky and sea. In fact, he was not very pleased with the picture himself. In a note dated 1859, he wrote: «My picture is full of mistakes, there is no doubt that my dreams are much better. There are too many details and nothing which captures the essence of Brittany: besides, the colors and light leave much to be desired.»

No doubt for this reason Baudelaire, does not dwell on the picture in his article on the Salon, but speaks at some length about Boudin's studies (not exhibited but which he had seen at Honfleur), «so rapidly and so faithfully sketched from those most fleeting and elusive shapes and colors, the waves and the clouds.» Baudelaire notes that on each study was «written in the margin the date, the time and the wind; thus for example: October 8, midday, north-west wind.» And it is the poet rather than the critic who gives such a lyrical description of Boudin's skies: «In the end all those clouds with their fantastic and luminous shapes, the chaotic darkness, the floating and intermingling masses of green and pink, the yawning furnaces, the firmaments of crushed, curled, or torn black or purple satin, the horizons draped with mourning or streaming with molten metal, all those depths and splendors went to my head like an intoxicating drink or the eloquence of opium.»

---

* See page 12.

Sailing Ship, c. 1880
Drawing and watercolor, 4³/₄ × 7¹/₁₆″ (12 × 18 cm)
Private collection

THE VAUBAN DOCK AT LE HAVRE, c. 1864–66
Oil on wood, $9\frac{1}{2}$″ × 13″ (24 × 33 cm)
Private collection

THE HARBOR AT ANTWERP, 1871
Oil on canvas, 15⅞″ × 25½″ (40.5 × 65.5 cm)
Louvre, Musée du Jeu de Paume, Paris

46

CANAL NEAR BRUSSELS, 1871
Oil on wood, 12½″ × 16¼″ (31.8 × 41.2 cm)
Private collection

47

The Harbor at Bordeaux, 1874
Oil on canvas, 27 3/4″ × 40 1/8″ (70.5 × 102 cm)
Louvre, Musée du Jeu de Paume, Paris

Three-Master Putting Out to Sea, c. 1876–78
Pencil, 6⁵/₁₆″ × 8¹/₄″ (16 × 21 cm)
Private collection

Sailboats, c. 1880–82
Pencil, 5¹/₂" × 7¹/₂" (14 × 19 cm)
Private collection

Fishermen and Boats, undated
Pencil, 5⁵/₁₆" × 8¹/₁₆" (13.5 × 20.5 cm)
Private collection

Baudelaire also noted, with some approval, «the absence of man» in the painter's studies. It is a remark that applies only to one of the two aspects of Boudin's work, and Baudelaire did not live long enough to appreciate the full extent of the artist's powers. In fact, Boudin seems to have fluctuated between spells of happiness, which made his friends regard him as a cheerful companion, and moods of depression, verging on disillusionment, which overcame him when he was alone and were recorded in his diary. The same dichotomy is reflected in his paintings: depicting either beaches, markets, and pilgrimages thronged with people, or nature devoid of all human presence, and the stretches of sky with no trace of land or sea that Baudelaire had admired.

Encouraged by his friends who begged him to return to Paris, Boudin moved into a studio at 8 boulevard Montmartre. A few months later he was again in Normandy, afterward visiting Quimper and returning to Le Havre. It was probably in 1860 that Boudin first stayed in Trouville, which would remain a favorite haunt for the rest of his life. It was already a fashionable seaside resort, a far cry from the «unknown beach» discovered by Alexandre Dumas thirty years earlier and which consisted of, as he wrote in his memoirs, «a few fishermen's cottages grouped on the right bank of the Touques, at the mouth of the river, between two ranges of hills.» At that time there was only a single inn, kept by Madame Oseraie and already frequented by painters like Decamps, Jadin, Mozin, and Huet. And it was at Trouville, in 1836, that Gustave Flaubert met his first love, the beautiful Elisa Schlesinger. But not until 1861 did Deauville (on the opposite bank of the river) become a truly fashionable resort under the aegis of the duc de Morny, half brother of Napoleon III.

Boudin spent the winter of 1861 in Paris. This time he lived near the Butte in Montmartre, at 66 rue Pigalle. «From our windows,» he wrote to his brother, «we can see the windmills on top of the Butte.» The pronoun indicates that he was not alone. In fact, he was living with a young Breton girl, Marie-Anne Guédès, who may well have had something to do with his growing love for Brittany, where from now on he would be a frequent visitor.

After a number of difficult months (for the few pictures he did manage to sell went for very low prices — he had agreed to paint pictures at seventy-five francs a dozen!), Boudin found a well-paid occupation working for Troyon, who had so many commissions he hired Boudin to square up his sketches for large compositions and sometimes even paint the sky. It was not very rewarding work, but Boudin was in no position to appear ungrateful. At the same time he was encouraged by the esteem and admiration in which he was held by painters whom he himself admired like his newfound friends Corot and Daubigny. It was Corot who exclaimed: «Boudin you are the king of the skies!»

Nevertheless, he could not go on working for Troyon forever. When summer came Boudin moved back to Honfleur where he lived at the Pavillon des Trente-six Marches, Rue de l'Homme-de-Bois. He did not return to Paris that year and he did not exhibit any pictures at the Salon. Instead, in the hope of earning some money, he and one of his painter friends, A. Dubourg, organized an exhibition at Caen in June 1862 where all the pictures were for sale. Boudin himself exhibited eleven paintings: still lifes, landscapes, market and pilgrimage scenes, and two seascapes. Here it should be noted that so far he had not set much store by his seascapes in his attempts to make his name. Unfortunately, the exhibition was a complete fiasco: not a single picture was sold, and poor Boudin wrote in a letter to his friend Martin: «I forgot to eat that day and the water of the Orne looked singularly tempting.»

LADY IN WHITE ON THE BEACH AT TROUVILLE, 1869
Oil on cardboard, $19^5/_{16}'' \times 12^5/_8''$ (49 $\times$ 32 cm)
Musée des Beaux-Arts André Malraux, Le Havre

Two Breton Countrymen Playing Bagpipes, undated
Pencil, 7⁷/₈″ × 10¹/₄″ (20 × 26 cm)
Louvre, Cabinet des Dessins

Fishermen on the Shore and Ships at Anchor, undated
Pencil, 3³/₄" × 5³/₁₆" (9.5 × 13.2 cm)
Private collection

55

RACES AT DEAUVILLE, 1866. Watercolor, 8″ × 12¼″ (19.5 × 30.5 cm)
Collection: Mr. and Mrs. Paul Mellon

TROUVILLE UNDER THE SECOND EMPIRE

A new figure had appeared in Boudin's life: Johann Barthold Jongkind. He is an interesting painter who merits a brief digression. According to Georges Jean-Aubry, Boudin's biographer, the two painters met through Monet in 1862, a statement that is repeated by John Rewald in his «History of Impressionism.» In her biography of Jongkind, however, Victorine Hefting says that Boudin and Jongkind met in 1860, while Jongkind first got to know Monet at the end of September 1862. She quotes a letter dated September 16, 1862, where Boudin asked Jongkind to come to Trouville. In any case, Jongkind and Boudin were certainly together at Trouville that summer as can be seen from the works by both painters dated 1862: Jongkind's *Trouville, Low Tide* and Boudin's *The Jetty at Trouville.**

Jongkind, who had been living in France since 1846, was then forty-three. Although he had not yet completely revealed the freedom of expression that would make him a precursor of Impressionism — and he had a great influence on Claude Monet as that artist was the first to acknowledge — Jongkind's watercolors already show the terse, rapid treatment of color and line that would earn him the reputation of being slipshod, although it was the most distinctive feature of his style. Like Turner, however, he never wanted to exhibit or sell his watercolors. And yet it was in this medium that he was most daring. Then, too, it most clearly reflected his anxious nature. All his life he was a victim of psychiatric problems, which were exacerbated by his alcoholism. It seems very likely that Jongkind's work encouraged Boudin to adopt a greater freedom in his painting technique. His drawing becomes more spontaneous, his style less stilted, and his colors brighter. It was the beginning of a successful time, the first major period of the *Beach Scenes.*

At the beginning of 1863 Boudin married Marie-Anne Guédès. They set up house in Paris, at 27 avenue Trudaine. Boudin sent *The Harbor at Honfleur* to the Salon, where he was to exhibit his work almost every year. In June he lost his father, the old sailor Léonard-Sébastien Boudin. And during the summer he paid his usual visit to the Normandy coast.

What fascinated Boudin at Trouville and Deauville was not so much the sea and the ships but the groups of people sitting on the sand or strolling along the beach: fine ladies in crinolines twirling their parasols, pompous gentlemen in top hats, children and little dogs playing on the sand. In the harmony of the colors of the elegant clothes, he found a contrast to the delicacy of his skies, which always took up at least two-thirds if not three-quarters of the picture. Sometimes he combined a beach scene and detailed view of the sea in the same composition, as in *The Beach at Trouville,*** where the groups seated by the water fill roughly the same amount of space as the sailing ships out at sea. But in most cases the beach scene is the main subject, either because the painter has chosen an unusual motif like the beach hut being transported by horse and cart in *On the Beach at Trouville,**** or because he makes a group the center of the picture as in *Empress Eugénie at Trouville.*

The enormous number of drawings, sketches, and watercolor or pastel studies left by Boudin show how greatly he was obsessed by the theme of the seaside. The often rapid sketches reveal his sureness of touch and skill as a colorist. The watercolors of the seaside, where the pencil lines can still be seen beneath the fluid colors, are among Boudin's most

---

* See page 19.   ** See page 15.   *** See page 18.

Boats, Low Tide, undated
Pencil with colored highlights
Louvre, Cabinet des Dessins, Paris

HIGH SEAS, 1872–76
Oil on canvas, 12⅝″ × 18⅛″ (32 × 47 cm)
Private collection

Sky Study, c. 1880. Pencil with colored highlights
Louvre, Cabinet des Dessins, Paris

attractive works, and the ones most indicative of his sensitivity and spontaneity. Moreover, they provide us with a precious glimpse of the way in which fashionable society spent the summer.

Boudin himself liked to spend summer on the coast and winter in Paris where he never stayed very long at the same address. Probably for reasons of economy he only rented an apartment for the winter months. At the beginning of 1864 he was living at 15 rue Durantin; by the end of the year he had moved to 31 rue Fontaine-Saint-Georges. Gradually, however, he was becoming more prosperous. He had begun to have some success with his *Beach Scenes* and was finding dealers who were interested in his work. Troyon bought a number of pastels from him. By this time Boudin was not only a master of composition but an enchanting and subtle colorist. All the pictures of 1864 bear the mark of this new harmony, including *The Beach at Villerville, Approaching Storm, On the Beach at Dieppe,** and, among the *Beaches at Trouville*, the one in the Louvre Museum, and the *Beach Scene* in the Mellon Collection.

Boudin was greatly affected by the death of Troyon in 1865. He missed him more as a friend than as a painter, for he had not particularly admired Troyon's last work or the frenzied production that left him no time to rest. Friendships were always important for Boudin, particularly with the painters who, by encouraging his work, helped him to retain confidence in himself. After Corot and Daubigny, Boudin became friends with Ribot, Courbet, and Whistler. The last two went to spend the summer in Trouville where they thought nothing of using their own prestige to find buyers for Boudin's pictures.

Altogether it was a fruitful summer for Boudin and the year 1865 saw some of his most successful paintings, including the *Concert at the Casino at Deauville*, which he exhibited at the Salon, *On the Beach at Sunset*, and countless *Beaches at Trouville* in oils, watercolors, and pastels.** By this time the seaside had become the major theme in Boudin's paintings. It was the subject that would bring him belated celebrity and which future generations would prefer to his landscapes. Even in 1865, he was beginning to be known as « the painter of beaches » by both collectors and dealers. Boudin was not altogether pleased. He went on working intermittently at Trouville and Deauville, but he was becoming increasingly attracted by Brittany where he found a new delight in painting the typical villages and their inhabitants.

On his return from a visit to Faou, Landernau, and Plougastel, he wrote in a letter to his friend Martin (August 28, 1867): « The beach at Trouville that I used to love so much seemed on my return no more than a hideous masquerade. One would almost have to be a genius to make anything out of that crowd of affected idlers. After spending a month with these peasants inured to backbreaking labor in the fields, black bread, and water, the sight of the horde of gilded parasites with their triumphant airs seems somehow pitiful, and one feels almost ashamed at painting the idle rich. » It is easy to imagine Eugène Boudin sitting on his little folding chair in a secluded corner of the beach in front of the tiny easel that he used for sketching outside (and which can still be seen in the Vieux Honfleur Museum), and grumbling about the « gilded parasites » — who incidentally would continue to provide him with material for a great many masterpieces, like *The Beach at Trouville*** which he sent to the Salon in 1867, and which was one of the twelve *Beach Scenes* painted during the summer when he was in such a bad temper.

---

* See front cover.   ** See pages 14, 20, and 26 to 31.   *** See page 39.

FROM CAMARET TO ROTTERDAM

Boudin, who had enjoyed a certain amount of success at the World Exhibition of 1867, organized an auction of his work in Paris on March 25, 1868. The result this time was far better than he expected. «Our little sketches done on the beach,» he wrote the next day, «have increased in value relatively much more than the seascapes. The pastels which are so difficult to sell have nearly all been bought by painters.» He also exhibited at Le Havre with Courbet, Daubigny, Manet, and Monet. There, too, his pictures received favorable notices and the *Beach at Trouville* earned him a silver medal. (Selection committees in the provinces, following the example of Paris, had adopted the ridiculous system of distributing medals like the awards given in the trade to camembert or mustard.)

The next year some of Boudin's works were exhibited at Pau and Roubaix and the circle of his buyers continued to increase. The consul of Baden-Württemberg at Le Havre, G. Rosenlecker, commissioned two decorative panels for his château at Bourdainville in Normandy. In order to have more space, Boudin hired a large studio at 32 rue Saint-Lazare. The decoration of the château dining room comprised a series of compositions: *Perspective of a Park, Partridge Shooting on the Cliff, The Roe Deer Covert, The Fountain with Flowers, Still Life with Parrots*, and *Still Life with a Straw Hat.* Boudin took great care over the execution of the paintings; he was possibly even overmeticulous. In any case, he wase never at his best with subjects of this kind. At the same time his seascapes and beaches were finding new buyers: dealers like his friend Martin, one Hagerman, and in particular a Belgian named Gauchez who, by his repeated purchases, allowed Boudin to forget his financial worries for a number of years.

During the summer of 1869 Boudin worked energetically on the Normandy coast and in Brittany (Daoulas, Landernau, Plougastel, l'Hôpital-Camfrout, and Portrieux), returning with thirty canvases or small panels (for Boudin preferred painting on wood to canvas). The pictures include *Beach Scene, Lady in White on the Beach at Trouville,** and watercolors like *Market in a Village Square.*

During the summer of 1870 Boudin traveled further than usual along the coast, from Cape Camaret in Finistère to Berck, Etaples, and Dunkirk. However, war had broken out and he was again beset by financial difficulties. Who wanted to buy pictures in those troubled times? Gauchez, who owed him money, suggested that he should come to Belgium. Boudin arrived in Brussels on December 12, taking rooms in the district of Saint-Gilles, first at 69 rue de Mérode and then at 74 rue de Hollande.

Boudin was delighted to meet up with an old friend, Antoine Vollon (1833–1900), a former pupil of Ribot whose still lifes and views of Antwerp and the banks of the Seine were very popular at the time. Boudin himself, always rather slow to get used to new landscapes, did not particularly like the surroundings of Brussels. The only things this lover of harbors and markets found to paint were the docks, a neighboring canal,** and the old fish market.

He therefore decided to explore the country, finding, especially in Antwerp, a number of subjects that proved to be valuable additions to his repertoire. After a brief return to Le Havre in April 1871 to visit his sick mother — she died at the beginning of June — he went back to Brussels and then in July spent six weeks with his friend Vollon in Antwerp. It was the first of several visits, and Boudin made countless sketches that would

---

* See pages 32 and 53.   ** See page 47.

CAMARET, 1872
Oil on canvas, 21 1/8″ × 35″ (53.6 × 89 cm)
Private collection, USA

provide the basis for almost forty pictures, some of them among the most beautiful he ever painted. One of his favorite scenes recurs in *Antwerp, the Scheldt and the Quays*, but at the same time he found in the northern skies colors that were very different from the ones he had been used to over the Channel, for example the putty color in the picture of the *The Harbor at Antwerp.* *

It was about this time that Boudin began to complain of the facial neuralgia from which he would often suffer as he grew older. Nevertheless, he went on working as hard as ever. He spent the autumn in Brittany and returned to Paris in December. From now on his usual tour of the French coast was completed by a stay in Antwerp, which he visited every year until 1876. In 1872, however, most of Boudin's painting was done in Brittany: over forty pictures, as compared with some fifteen in Trouville, Honfleur, Le Havre, and Sainte-Adresse, as well as seven in Atwerp. (The figures are only a rough estimate as a great many of Boudin's works are not dated.) For the time being he was more interested in ships and harbors than in beach scenes. He painted seascapes at Brest, Camaret, ** Paimpol, and Portrieux, besides pictures of markets like *Le Faou, Market Day*. In 1873 Boudin visited another two cities with harbors, Bordeaux in France and Rotterdam in Holland.

THE BEGINNINGS OF IMPRESSIONISM

The year 1874 is important in the history of painting. It was the year of the first exhibition given by the group of Impressionists, although they were not yet known by that name. At the instigation of Claude Monet, thirty artists united in their hostility toward the principle of official Salons and selection committees, had founded the « Co-operative Company of Painters, Sculptors, Engravers, etc.» Nadar had lent them a showroom at 35 boulevard des Capucines. Beside the painters who would become famous—Monet, Renoir, Cézanne, Degas, Sisley, Pissarro, and Berthe Morisot—the first group included the names of Lépine, Guillaumin, Bracquemond, Cals, and de Nittis, not to mention another seventeen artists who are almost unknown today. Boudin was invited to the exhibition and sent three pictures, one of Finistère, *Le Toulinguet, Camaret Coast*, and two of the Côtes-du-Nord, both of them views of *The Shore at Portrieux*. He also exhibited six pastel studies (including four skies) and four watercolors with the same title: *The Beach at Trouville*.

Until 1886 another seven exhibitions, not all with works by the same artists, constituted the main manifestation of the movement that would soon be known as Impressionism. Boudin, however, only took part in the first exhibition in 1874. It is true that all the artists in the group were far from showing the same aesthetic principles and that few of them possessed a vision and technique that was genuinely Impressionist. And what of Boudin himself?

To answer the question we must look at the painting he was doing at the time, for example, *The Harbor at Bordeaux* *** dated 1874. The picture, acquired by the French State in 1899, was not shown at the Impressionist exhibition, in spite of what has sometimes

---

See page 46.   ** See page 63.   *** See page 48.

64

A COUNTRY VILLA, 1885
Oil on wood, 12″ × 15¾″ (30.5 × 40 cm)
Collection: Mr. and Mrs. Paul Mellon

ROTTERDAM, THE BRIDGE, 1876
Oil on canvas, 17³/₄″ × 25⁵/₈ (45 × 65 cm)
Private collection

MARKET AT TROUVILLE, 1876
Oil on wood, 13″ × 16⅛″ (33 × 41 cm)
Private collection

REGATTAS AT ANTWERP, c. 1880
Oil on wood panel, $8\frac{1}{4}'' \times 14\frac{9}{16}''$ (21 × 37 cm)
Musée Eugène Boudin, Honfleur

been stated, notably in the official «Catalogue of Impressionist Paintings, Pastels and Sculptures» published in 1959 by the Louvre Museum. The picture could not have been shown there for the simple reason that the exhibition lasted from April 15 to May 15, whereas Boudin did not go to Bordeaux until October. The picture itself has nothing Impressionist about it. The wharfs, the water, the ships, the distant city, and the sky are all painted in different shades of gray and brownish gray that have nothing in common with the Impressionist palette. The whole style is fundamentally different. Another painting dated 1874, *Surroundings of Portrieux*, from the former Durand-Ruel Collection, has a different range of colors with its brown earth and glowering stormy sky, but is still a long way from the Impressionist technique. (The picture may have been shown at the first exhibition under the title *The Shore at Portrieux.*) It is interesting to note, and typical of Boudin's independence, that in later years a great many of his works did show distinctly Impressionist characteristics of color and brushwork although he himself no longer belonged to the group.

Throughout his life Boudin went his own way without paying any attention to what other artists were doing, stubbornly clinging to his own view of painting in spite of success or failure. Perhaps such perseverance was inherited from his seafaring ancestors: the need to steer a straight course against wind and tide. Boudin was always lucid in his judgments of people and things; he often complained of the harshness and injustice of life, but the pictures he produced were always serene. He was never happier than when painting, and nothing could deflect him from carrying out his work. We have seen his irritation with the idle rich at Trouville; we know he did not like Antwerp, but painted some marvelous landscapes there; just as in 1875 he wrote that he was not fond of the wharfs of Bordeaux, «a city as unattractive as Le Havre,» yet he went back there for a number of years, producing between 1874 and 1876 over seventy-five pictures, mainly of the despised harbor and wharfs. We have to distinguish between the painter and the man: ambivalent in his perception of the world around him, Boudin knew how to separate the wheat from the tares and he never showed in his canvases anything less than an enchanted vision.

It was a bad period for painting, or rather for painters. «An unprecendented crisis,» wrote Boudin at the end of 1876, and in March 1877: «The public no longer seems to be interested in anything.» He thought that the crisis was likely to last a number of years. To understand it, one should remember the economic situation of the time and also bear in mind that it coincided with the disappearance of some of the great names in nineteenth century painting: Millet and Corot died in 1875, Diaz in 1876, Courbet in 1877, and Daubigny in 1878. They were all friends of Boudin and he was very distressed by their loss. On closer examination we can see that the crisis only affected a certain category of artists, those who, like Boudin, were not in receipt of official honors. And the «Impressionist revolution» had not yet altered the taste of the public. At a time when Boudin could not sell his work and Renoir was painting portraits for 100 francs each, while eleven of his pictures left the auction rooms for a total of 500 francs, Alexandre Cabanel's *Florentine Poet* was sold for 56,000 francs in 1876 and Léon Bonnat's *Italian Dancers* went for 75,000 francs the next year. Cabanel, of course, had been a member of the Institut de France since 1863 and Bonnat would be elected in 1881.

In spite of his despondency, Boudin went on working as he traveled from Brittany to Normandy and Berck, and then on to Holland where he stayed in Dordrecht, Rotterdam, and Scheveningen. His morale may have been low but his painting had never been better, as we can see from the *Market at Trouville** or *Rotterdam, The Bridge.***

In 1878 Boudin moved back to Paris where he lived at 54 rue Lamartine. In spite of the dearth of buyers, he decided to try his luck in the auction rooms. The sale was held in March 1879 and included thirty-eight pictures, some twenty watercolors, and a number of seaside sketches. The bidding was not very encouraging, with the pictures reaching a maximum of 400 francs. The ones that sold best were scenes of markets or washerwomen, while the drawings went for an average of 25 francs each. The total brought in 6,000 francs. It was not very much, but it was better than another sale he organized jointly with Armand Gautier in Le Havre in July of the same year. Gautier did not sell anything, and Boudin, represented by fourteen paintings of his favorite sites in Normandy and Holland, only sold four at prices ranging from 85 to 210 francs. No wonder he was astonished the next year when he managed to sell a painting for 900 francs. It was the first indication of a more prosperous period brought about by the appearance in his life of a man who was already well known to painters for his farsightedness and generosity — Durand-Ruel.

THE PAINTER AND THE CRITICS

After having been one of the first to defend the Barbizon group, Paul Durand-Ruel (1831–1922) had bought the paintings of the new generation although they were almost universally condemned at the time. He had exhibited Manet, Sisley, and Pissarro in London in 1872 and in 1876 he organized the second Impressionist exhibition at his Paris gallery in 11 rue Le Peletier. It was a lucky day for Eugène Boudin when Durand-Ruel came to visit him on February 5, 1881. He wanted to see all the painter's work and, as he had done for Manet a number of years before, he finally bought the entire contents of the studio. In a letter Boudin wrote that Durand-Ruel had also asked him to « work only for him. » (It should, however, be pointed out that no exclusive rights contract is to be found in the Durand-Ruel archives, something which would have been against his usual practice.)

Financially reassured, Boudin began to regain confidence. He wrote that he was « working like a maniac. » « I am so busy painting I no longer have time to breathe. » The picture he sent to the Salon in 1881, *On the River Meuse at Rotterdam*, won him the princely award of a bronze medal. Gradually, however, his name was becoming known. Durand-Ruel did not neglect him. When he opened a new gallery at 9 boulevard de la Madeleine it was inaugurated on March 1, 1883 with a Boudin exhibition: one hundred and fifty pictures and a series of pastel and watercolor sketches. The subjects included views of Brittany, the coast of Normandy and the Pas-de-Calais, as well as Bordeaux, Antwerp, and Holland.

---

* See page 67.   ** See page 66.

Market Scene, undated
Pencil
Louvre, Cabinet des Dessins, Paris

71

At last the critics began to take an interest. Boudin was praised in all the newspapers: « This is the forty-eighth article about me! » he exclaimed. Surprisingly, he was appreciated for the very qualities that had earlier been condemned in the Impressionists. « The painting is light, » wrote Philippe Burty in « La République Française, » « revealing the colored transparency of the air and the substance of the objects. » De Fourcaud in « Le Gaulois » saw in Boudin « one of the most sincere, subtle and best landscape artists of the present day, » and he also noted: « If there is anyone who only trusts his immediate impression, immediately recorded, to render what he sees, it is M. Boudin. » Here the journalist was in agreement with Boudin himself, who twenty-five years earlier had taught the young Monet: « You must be absolutely determined to retain the first impression, which is the correct one. » Gustave Geffroy had not been wrong in recognizing Boudin as one of the « immediate precursors of Impressionism, » and it is he who has left us the most graphic description of the 1883 Boudin exhibition: « These paintings (mainly seascapes) reproduce atmospheric conditions, the play of light on beaches and wet rocks, shifting mists, stormy skies, the uncertainty of marine horizons. »

The picture Boudin sent to the Salon that year (two views of Le Havre) won him a silver medal. Although he was beginning to become famous and enjoying a period of financial prosperity, Boudin clung to his old habits. He continued to visit Holland and the Normandy coast and the pictures he painted at Trouville that summer were not necessarily all beach scenes; he also produced some pure landscapes — always somewhat of a rarity in his work — like the Scene along the Touques River, now in an English collection.

Boudin was at last in a position to afford his own house, and in 1884 he built a small villa at Deauville, which he christened the « Villa des Ajoncs » (Gorse Villa). This did not prevent him from visiting Holland where he painted forty-five pictures of Dordrecht in the same year. The subjects include the banks of the Meuse, the harbor, the canals, the windmills, and views of the town with the cathedral tower.

In 1885, whether out of curiosity or a need to find new subjects, Boudin decided to visit the Mediterranean coast for the first time. He must have been somewhat disoriented at first by the strong light to which his palette was not accustomed. Nevertheless, he returned several times during the next few years and painted a series of pictures at Villefranche, Antibes, Beaulieu, Nice, and Juan-les-Pins.

Although he no longer belonged to the Impressionist group, Boudin agreed to send twenty-three works to the major exhibition organized by Durand-Ruel in April 1886 in New York at the National Academy of Design, under the auspices of the American Art Association and entitled « The Impressionists of Paris. » The catalogue had a preface by Théodore Duret (1836–1927), a well-known collector and expert on Impressionism. In fact, only a few among the painters of the 312 pictures exhibited in New York could really be described as Impressionist: alongside Monet, Renoir, Sisley, Pissarro, and Berthe Morisot, we find names like Caillebotte, Flameng, Jean-Paul Laurens, and Roll, as well as others who are almost unknown today. By this time there were hardly any pure Impressionists left among the seventeen participants in the group's latest Paris exhibition in the same year. What was significant was that Seurat exhibited his Sunday Afternoon on the Island of « La Grande Jatte »: a new school had come into being that became known as Neo-Impressionism.

Although Boudin is mainly famous for the Trouville beach scenes and to a lesser extent his seascapes and harbors, he nevertheless painted a great many other subjects. The fact that some of them were frequently repeated shows that in his eyes they were scarcely less interesting than the views of the seaside. He seems never to have tired of certain themes like the *Washerwomen on the Touques River,** which he had been painting for over twenty years and would continue to paint until the end of his life. Another favorite scene was the market-place, like the fish market in Trouville and others in Fervaques, Honfleur, and Brittany. Then, too, he made so many *Sketches of Cattle* that it is hard to imagine what he intended to do with them. During the eighties alone he produced over one hundred seventy-five paintings of meadows, not to mention several hundred drawings, gouaches, and watercolors. Apparently somebody must have appreciated all these cattle, or perhaps Boudin himself found them a welcome change from his usual seaside studies. It may be, however, that as a seaman's son and a painter of seascapes, Boudin regarded the land like the French sailors who refer to terra firma as « le plancher des vaches » (the cattle deck).

It would be wrong to think that Boudin was only interested in beaches crowded with elegant bathers who never venture into the water. He often painted deserted shores seen at low tide, sometimes with a glimpse of a distant fisherman, and where the effects of sky and sea are the main subject of the picture, as in *Honfleur, Low Tide.* In fact, during his last years Boudin painted hardly any « beach scenes, » and the ones dating from the sixties were probably the best he ever did.

Boudin frequently painted village squares and farmyards, and sometimes churches and church interiors. He also made a great many sketches of groups of peasants at pilgrimages and fairs. He always liked painting the inhabitants of the villages as well as the buildings. But, as already pointed out, he was not particularly interested in nature for its own sake, although he did paint one or two beautiful pictures of landscapes devoid of people, and his drawings include large charcoal landscapes and studies of trees that are far more than mere sketches or notes.

Boudin painted very few portraits, besides the one of this father and another of a lady presumed to be his wife. His work contains only a small number of close-ups of groups where the subjects can be identified. Even in *A Country Villa*** of 1885, the house is given more importance than the two women and the little girl in the foreground, and in *The Dubois Family on the Terrace of the Pavillon Jeanne at Deauville**** of 1887, it is by no means certain whether or not the figure in white at the extreme right is indeed Boudin's wife.

It is not surprising that in the course of fifty years Boudin's painting should sometimes have been uneven, with certain periods more successful than others, but it does seem as if his best pictures, the ones that enchant us today, were not necessarily the ones that were most appreciated or found buyers in his own lifetime. His marvelous *Beach Scenes* were not as popular as the *Cattle in Pasture,* the subject that had made Rosa Bonheur famous, and Boudin's cattle scenes never fetched prices as high as hers. No wonder the artist was sometimes perplexed and uncertain as to which path to pursue.

---

* See page 83.   ** See page 65.   *** See page 77.

Fishermen's Cabins at Etretat, undated
Pencil
Louvre, Cabinet des Dessins, Paris

LADY WITH A PARASOL, c. 1880
Oil on wood panel, $4^{15}/_{16}'' \times 6^{7}/_{8}''$ (12.5 × 17.5 cm)
Musée Eugène Boudin, Honfleur

THE DUBOIS FAMILY ON THE TERRACE
OF THE PAVILION JEANNE AT DEAUVILLE, 1887
Oil on wood, $13^{3}/_{4}'' \times 10^{7}/_{16}$ (35 × 26.5 cm)
Private collection
▷

VENICE, THE SALUTE AND THE CANAL GRANDE, 1895
Oil on canvas, 14$^1/_8$" × 22$^7/_8$" (36 × 58 cm). Private collection

VILLEFRANCHE, THE BAY, 1892. Oil on canvas, 19⁵/₈″ × 29¹/₈″ (50 × 74 cm)
Private collection

ETRETAT, THE UPSTREAM CLIFF, 1890. Oil on canvas, $18\frac{1}{8}'' \times 25\frac{5}{8}''$ (46 × 65 cm)
Private collection

At last, however, came the kind of success that Boudin with his inveterate pessimism had not dared to hope for. On April 19, 1888, he sold sixty pictures, thirty pastels, and ten watercolors in an auction at the Hotel Drouot. And at the Salon in the same year, the State, which had already bought one of his works at the 1886 Salon — *A Squall* (Morlaix Museum) — acquired for the Luxembourg Museum *The Russian Corvette in the Eure Docks.*

This swing in favor of Boudin's painting, both on the part of collectors and in official circles, became more pronounced the following year with a new exhibition presented by Durand-Ruel. In the meantime, however, Boudin had been plunged into sadness by the death of his wife, Marie-Anne, on March 24, 1889.

It is hoped that he was somewhat comforted, a few months later, by the success of his exhibition that opened on July 8. It comprised eigthy-nine paintings, a series of pastels, and nine charcoal drawings. The drawings were of landscapes of the Côte de Grâce at Honfleur and the fact that he chose to exhibit them at Durand-Ruel's suggests that Boudin attached a certain importance to them. Today they are the least known aspect of his art and reveal not only his great qualities as a draftsman but also a deep feeling for nature. The exhibition received enthusiastic notices and a large number of pictures were sold. Boudin met with equal success at Bordeaux where he exhibited seascapes, and at the 1889 World Exhibition where he was awarded a gold medal.

So many commissions now began to pour in that Boudin could not find time to meet them all. In 1890 he sent paintings to the Salon of the Société Nationale des Beaux-Arts, founded the preceding year, and to the « Amis des Arts » exhibition in Le Havre where all his pictures were sold. He also worked for Durand-Ruel who was organizing an exhibition of thirteen of Boudin's pictures at Chase's Gallery in Boston, in May, while exhibiting Boudin for the third time at his Paris gallery, in December, together with a group of painters and sculptors, including Fantin-Latour, Eugène Carrière, Jacques-Emile Blanche, Rodin, Dalou, and Constantin Meunier.

Boudin was thus obliged to renew his stock of pictures, once more visiting the familiar places between Deauville and Dunkirk where his favorite shores were to be found. At Etretat he painted twenty pictures, including *The Upstream Cliff,** and at the same time he went out into the countryside to paint pure landscapes like *The Meadow near Caudebec.*** The same summer he traveled in Holland and once more visited the South of France.

VENETIAN INTERLUDES

In March 1891 there was another Boudin exhibition at Durand-Ruel's with thirty-four paintings, a number of pastel studies and many drawings. The pastel studies were mainly of seascapes and skies, the areas of sky that Boudin treated as subjects in their own right and which can be seen in the Honfleur museum with titles like *White Clouds Over the Estuary, Fair Weather, White Clouds,* or *Blue Sky, White Clouds.* The drawings were of beaches, seascapes, groups of fisherwomen, markets, pilgrimages, and interiors of Breton farms.

---

* See page 80.   ** See page 85.

DUNKIRK, ENTRANCE TO THE HARBOR, 1889
Oil on canvas, 18¼″ × 25¾″ (46.5 × 65.5 cm)
Private collection

The 1891 Salon showed ten works by Boudin, all of them subjects from the Channel coast, while the eight paintings he exhibited at the 1892 Salon were exclusively views of the South of France: three of Beaulieu and five of Villefranche. Gustave Geffroy wrote of them in his review of the Salon in «La Vie artistique»: They are «executed in the subtle style of patches of color bathed in gray light that is characteristic of the artist, and that is so good at showing, in the transparent distance, buildings, boats, the eddies in the water and the movements of the clouds.» The southern light a «gray light?» Surely the critic must have made a mistake. But no, Boudin never really liked bright sunshine as we shall see a little later in the context of Italy. The State bought *Villefranche the Bay*,* a subject that occurs several times among the twenty-five pictures Boudin painted in 1892, which include other views of Villefranche like *The Bay of Saint-Jean*, *The Citadel* and *The Fleet*, as well as paintings of the wharfs and streets of the town and the surrounding mountains.

Boudin had never been further north than Holland or further south than the Mediterranean coast of France when suddenly, in the spring of 1892, at the age of sixty-seven, he decided to visit Italy for the first time. He stayed in Venice and liked what he saw for he returned on two occasions. For some reason, however, he painted very little during his first stay in the city. He may very well have made a number of studies and drawings, but he did not exhibit any pictures of Venice in the Salon before 1897.

In October 1892 Boudin received the Legion of Honor, which was bestowed on him by Puvis de Chavannes at the request of Léon Bourgeois, the Minister of Public Education. Over a year earlier, Boudin, who said that he was «sufficiently rewarded by the approval of the public,» had taken steps to have the ribbon given to Jongkind. «It seemed to me,» he wrote to Alfred Stevens, «that that master should take precedence over me.» But it was too late: Jongkind died of a stroke in 1891.

In 1893 Boudin continued to live in Normandy, and then, because his health was not good, decided to spend the winter on the Mediterranean. He painted over fifty pictures at Golfe-Juan, Juan-les-Pins and especially Antibes and its surroundings. He returned to Venice in June 1894 but scarcely painted any more than on his first visit. He came back for the last time in May 1895 and spent two months in the city. This time he did an enormous amount of work, although he wrote to his brother Louis: «I wish I was twenty years younger to be able to make my stay worthwhile for myself and for art, but I feel exhausted by the hard task of painting.» It was indeed a hard task for that year, in addition to some seventy pictures painted in Normandy, he produced seventy-five views of Venice.

Inevitably, Boudin painted *The Salute and the Canal Grande*,** the Campanile and the Doges' Palace, San Giorgio Maggiore and the Giudecca, but he also portrayed the less familiar small canals, as well as the Riva degli Schiavoni complete with fishing boats and sailing ships, gondolas and even steamers of which he said that they «stain the marble palaces.» The style of the paintings differs little from Boudin's treatment of the French coast. There is the same spontaneity and delicacy and, more surprisingly, the same range of colors. In the artist's eyes the skies of the Adriatic were very similar to the skies over the Channel. In fact, he wrote on June 20, 1895: «I am busy painting views of Venice, a superb town as I have no need to tell you, but somewhat disguised by the usual painters

---

* See page 79.   ** See page 78.

THE MEADOW NEAR CAUDEBEC, 1890
Oil on canvas, 18 1/8″ × 25 5/8″ (46 × 65 cm)
Private collection

of the area who have to some extent disfigured it by making it appear as a region warmed by the hottest suns. ... Venice on the other hand, like all luminous regions, is gray in color, the atmosphere is soft and misty and the sky is decked with clouds just like the sky over Normandy or Holland.» (Letter to Paul Durand-Ruel, lent to me by Mr. Charles Durand-Ruel, who kindly gave me access to his grandfather's archives).

DEAUVILLE FOR THE LAST TIME

Boudin was tired and listless. Returning to Deauville in 1896 he did not find the hoped-for benefits from what he called «a little blow from the Channel.» What he needed was something even more invigorating and it looks as if he may have found it in painting *Gale at Le Havre. (Petit-Palais Museum)*. Nevertheless, Boudin was worried about his declining strength. He exhibited at the «Amis des Arts» in Le Havre, but did not send anything to the Paris Salon. And 1897 was the last time he was represented there with two views of Deauville (*The Shore* and *The Marsh*), two seascapes, and eight small sketches of Venice in the same frame.

The same year Boudin returned to Brittany in May, visiting Pointe du Raz, Brest, Douarnenez, Pont-Aven, Belle Isle, Nantes, and Saint-Nazaire. Afterward he went back to Deauville where he spent the summer. There and at Trouville he painted some forty pictures: of the harbor, the docks, the ships, and his last *Beach Scene*.

Boudin also made a lithograph for an album by L. Roger-Milès, «Art et nature» (published in 1897 by G. Boudet). The print was entitled *Mathurins* and shows a group of sailors on a wharf. It was an unusual work for Boudin, who had never taken more than a passing interest in lithography. He had used the technique for the first time in 1851 when he produced a lithograph of a drawing by A. Couveley, then director of Le Havre Museum. The only other print he is known to have made was an etching of a *Seascape* in 1898, published in «L'Estampe et l'affiche,» a review edited by Clément Janin and Mellerio.

Boudin spent the winter in Paris in his studio in the Place Vintimille. It was a bad winter. Boudin was ill and could scarcely eat. He probably did not know that he was suffering from cancer of the stomach. «I am extremely weak,» he wrote to his brother on February 27, 1898, «every movement tires me ... and yet I was able to paint today and found it a great relief. I do not expect to stay very long in Paris. The doctor wants me to go to the south to finish my convalescence beside the blue sea among the orange blossom.» Boudin accordingly went to Beaulieu where he stayed from April 5 to May 20, first in the Hôtel du Commerce and afterward in the Hôtel Beaurivage. «I am not painting any more,» he wrote on April 27, «I no longer have either the strength or the desire ...»

Yet he did take up his brushes again and returned to the «Baie des Fourmis», which he had often painted in former years. There are a number of paintings of that name, including one dated 1892 which is today in the Metropolitan Museum in New York. And it was *Beaulieu, Baie des Fourmis* which was his last picture, the only one he painted in 1898. It is executed in broad strokes, but the apparent freedom of the style does not conceal the fact that it is the last effort of a hand that has lost its energy.

In June Boudin was taken back to Deauville, to his house in Rue Olliffe. He felt that his last days were at hand, he wanted to spend them near the shore he had loved for so long. It was there at dawn on August 8, 1898, that the eyes of Eugène Boudin closed forever, those blue eyes that seemed to reflect all the skies he had ever painted.

The funeral took place in Paris on August 12, at the Church of La Trinité. He is buried in the Saint-Vincent cemetery at Montmartre, beside his wife, Marie-Anne.

★

It was not long before exhibitions began to be organized in honor of the late painter. Durand-Ruel showed about fifty of Boudin's works in his New York Fifth Avenue Gallery from December 15, 1898, to January 15, 1899. In Paris, at the initiative of the collector Gustave Cahen, Boudin's executor, and with the backing of a committee chaired by Léon Bourgeois, the Ecole des Beaux-Arts housed the largest Boudin exhibition that had ever been held, lasting from January 9 to 30, 1899. A total of 457 works were shown, 364 oil paintings, 73 pastels and 20 watercolors. The museums of Le Havre, Honfleur and Bordeaux lent pictures, as did many private collectors, including Constant Coquelin, Georges Feydeau, Rouart, and Aurelien Scholl. The exhibition provided a panorama of the painter's work, with pictures painted over a period of forty years, from 1857 to 1897.

Huge as the retrospective exhibition was, it only represented a small portion of Eugène Boudin's work. Robert Schmit, who wrote a « Catalogue raisonné » of it in 1973, painstakingly counted 3,651 oil paintings. And several hundred pictures discovered since will be listed in a supplement to the three large volumes. The number of watercolors, pastels, and drawings is even greater. The ones in private collections in France and abroad have never really been catalogued, but the Louvre Museum Cabinet des Dessins alone contains 5,887 in its portfolios. Others are to be found in a number of museums, notably at Le Havre and Honfleur, which at the same time possess large collections of Boudin's paintings.

The Le Havre Beaux-Arts Museum, to which the painter had bequeathed three pictures, was further enriched by a donation by Louis Boudin in 1899 of the paintings given him by his brother Eugène: sixty studies on canvas and one hundred and eighty on wood. In addition, the museum owns seventy of Boudin's gouaches and drawings, while the artist's legacy to the Honfleur Municipal Museum comprised twenty-eight paintings and twenty-four pastels.

Another museum in the same town, the Vieux-Honfleur Museum, was inaugurated on August 13, 1899, with an exhibition of regional painters and a whole room devoted to Boudin. On that occasion, Albert Sorel of the French Academy made a speech praising the Honfleur painter — a task for which he was not particularly well qualified, for although a native of Honfleur, he had little connection with art, being a distinguished diplomat, historian, and a professor at the School of Political Science.

Today thirty-eight towns in France and eighty abroad have works by Boudin in their museums. In spite of this, a considerable proportion of his work is not on show but remains confined to portfolios. These are the watercolors that are too vulnerable to the effects of light to be exhibited. They represent one of the most subtle and direct forms of expression of a painter who has been to lightly dismissed as a « minor master » and who might be better described as a *landscape intimist.*

The term «intimism» could be applied not only to the beach scenes where the presence of the figures makes the background of the sea seem less forbidding, but also to all the shores, harbors, and ships riding at anchor or plowing the sea beneath skies that appear to be constantly changing. For Boudin is able to make us share in the love with which he painted his seascapes, in that instant of perfect communion with the light in which they are suffused, by placing the spectator in an intimate relationship with the scenes he chooses to portray.

Thus, when he paints ships, it is unusual for him to show them far out at sea, carrying our thoughts toward distant horizons in the manner of the seventeenth-century Dutch seascape painters who have sometimes been described as his masters: the Van de Veldes, the Backhuysens, or the Flemish painter Van Eertvelt who excelled at painting storms. Although in his *Low Tides*, and especially in the *Sky Studies* admired by Baudelaire, Boudin takes a delight in nature for its own sake, so that the pictures sometimes contain not even a glimpse of the land, the seascapes usually show the outline of a cliff or a jetty or a lighthouse, as if the artist felt the need to place a tangible link between the spectator and infinity.

Blessed with a profound sense of equilibrium, both in his life and in his art, Eugène Boudin appears at his most typical when, from his dreams of the wide open spaces of the sea and the sky, his eyes open to evoke the presence of a human being.

JEAN SELZ

THREE-MASTER AND BOATS AT THE ENTRANCE OF A HARBOR IN NORMANDY, c. 1896
Oil on canvas, $25^{5}/_{8}'' \times 36^{1}/_{4}''$ (65 × 92 cm)
Musée Eugène Boudin, Honfleur

BIOGRAPHY

1824 Louis-Eugène Boudin was born at Honfleur on July 12, the son of Léonard-Sébastien Boudin, a sailor, and his wife Marie-Félicité.

1834 Cabin boy on his father's small boat, «Le Polichinelle.»

1835 The Boudin family moved to Le Havre. Eugène spent a year at a school run by priests.

1836 Worked as a clerk for the publisher-printer Joseph Morlent and afterward for the stationer Alphonse Lamasle. Eugène drew in his spare time.

1844 He opened a stationer's shop with a partner, Jean Acher. The two friends also framed pictures. They exhibited a number of canvases by painters who had come to work at Le Havre: Thomas Couture, Eugène Isabey, J.-F. Millet, and Constant Troyon. Millet corrected Boudin's first attempts at painting.

1846 Forced to sell his share in the business to avoid military service, Boudin broke off his partnership with Jean Acher. Determined to devote his time to painting, he set up a small studio on the Grand-Quai.

1847 First stay in Paris.

1849 Sent by Baron Taylor on a publicity tour for the benefit of poor artists and writers, he traveled through the north of France and Belgium, afterward returning to Le Havre.

1850 First known paintings. Exhibited for the first time at the Société des Amis des Arts in Le Havre. Sold two pictures.

1851 Le Havre municipality awarded him a grant for three years. He returned to Paris.

1852 Showed eleven pictures at Le Havre Museum biennial exhibition.

1854 Back in Le Havre. Stayed at Honfleur at the Saint-Siméon farm.

1855 Visited Brittany.

1857 Another visit to Brittany. Exhibited a number of pictures at the Concert Musard in Paris.

1858 Showed eleven pictures at the Société des Amis des Arts exhibition. Met the young Claude Monet and encouraged him to paint.

1859 Got to know Courbet and Baudelaire. First picture exhibited at the Salon des Artistes français: *The Pilgrimage at Sainte-Anne-la-Palud.* Baudelaire discussed it in his «Salon de 1859.» Boudin lived in Paris at 8 boulevard Montmartre.

1860 Visited Quimper, Le Havre, Honfleur, and Trouville.

1861 Spent the winter in Paris at 66 rue Pigalle. Worked for Troyon. Met Corot. Went to Honfleur for the summer.

1862 Unsuccessful exhibition and sale at Caen. Friendship with Jongkind.

1863 Married Marie-Anne Guédès. Lived in Paris at 27 avenue Trudaine. From now on exhibited almost every year at the Salon. Death of Boudin's father. Visited the Normandy coast, where he would return nearly every summer until the end of his life.

1864 Lived in Paris at 15 rue Durantin and afterward at 31 rue Fontaine-Saint-Georges.

1865 At Trouville, Courbet and Whistler found him buyers. *The Beach Scenes* met with success. Boudin was greatly affected by the death of Troyon.

1867 Took part in the World Exhibition. Stayed in Brittany.

1868 Organized a successful sale of his works in Paris. Also met with success at an exhibition in Le Havre. Worked in Brittany.

1869 Painted decorative panels for the Château of Bourdainville. Took a studio in Paris at 31 rue Saint Lazare. Exhibited at Pau and Roubaix. Stayed in Brittany. A Belgian collector, Gauchez, gave him a large number of commissions.

1870   Visited Camaret, Berck, Dunkirk, and, as usual, the Normandy coast. Went to Brussels in December.

1871   Lived in Brussels and Antwerp. Death of Boudin's mother. Spent the autumn in Brittany and December in Paris. Suffered from facial neuralgia.

1872   Visited Antwerp and Brittany.

1873   Went to Brittany, Antwerp, Rotterdam, and Bordeaux.

1874   Took part in the first Impressionist exhibition. Visited Brittany, Antwerp, and Bordeaux.

1875   Stayed in Belgium, Holland, Brittany, and Bordeaux.

1876   Visited Rotterdam and Bordeaux.

1878   Stayed in Berck and Camaret. Found a new studio in Paris at 54 rue Lamartine.

1879   Auctions in Paris and Le Havre. Visited Brest, Portrieux, Berk, Rotterdam, and Bordeaux. Exhibited at Le Havre.

1880   Went to Holland and Brittany. Again exhibited at Le Havre.

1881   Durand-Ruel became his main buyer. Visited Berck and Dordrecht.

1882   Went to Berck and Boulogne. Lived in Paris at 11 place Vintimille.

1883   Exhibition at Durand-Ruel's. Durand-Ruel also showed his pictures at an exhibition in Boston. Went to Brittany, Saint-Valéry-en-Caux, and Holland.

1884   Visited Dordrecht. Built the «Villa des Ajoncs» at Deauville.

1885   Went to Holland and for the first time visited the South of France where he stayed at Villefranche.

1886   Participated in an exhibition organized by Durand-Ruel in New York. At the Paris Salon, A Squall was bought by the State. Stayed in Holland.

1887   Went to Brittany. Exhibited at Le Havre.

1888   Successful sale at the Hôtel Drouot. At the Salon The Russian Corvette in the Eure Docks was bought by the State.

1889   Death of his wife Marie-Anne. Another exhibition at Durand-Ruel's. Took part in the World Exhibition and obtained a gold medal. Exhibited at Bordeaux. Stayed in Dunkirk.

1890   Spent June in the north. Stayed in Holland and the South of France. Exhibited at Le Havre (all his pictures were bought). Exhibited at the Salon of the Société Nationale des Beaux-Arts (where he continued to show pictures in future years). Third exhibition at Durand-Ruel's. Durand-Ruel also exhibited his pictures at Chase's Gallery in Boston.

1891   Fourth exhibition at Durand-Ruel's. Stayed in Brittany and the South of France.

1892   At the Salon, Villefranche the Bay was bought by the State. Boudin received the Legion of Honor. Visited Venice for the first time.

1893   Stayed in the South of France and Brittany.

1894   Second visit to Venice.

1895   Third visit to Venice, went on to the South of France.

1896   Exhibited at Le Havre. His health was declining. He sent nothing to the Salon.

1897   Traveled in Brittany from Brest to Saint-Nazaire. Exhibited his last picture at the Salon. As usual spent the summer in Normandy and the winter in Paris. Suffered from cancer of the stomach.

1898   Spent March to May in Beaulieu. Painted his last picture there. Returned to his house in Rue Olliffe at Deauville. Died there on August 8. The funeral was in Paris, at the Church of La Trinité. He was buried at the Saint-Vincent cemetery in Montmartre.
In December, a Boudin exhibition was held at Durand-Ruel's Gallery in New York.

1899   Major Boudin exhibition (457 works) at the Ecole des Beaux-Arts. In March, sale of the contents of Boudin's studio at the Hôtel Drouot (125 pictures, 98 watercolors, and 56 pastels).

1900   Inauguration of a bust of Eugène Boudin by Ernest Guilbert at Honfleur.

BIBLIOGRAPHY

ALEXANDRE, Arsène. *L'Œuvre d'Eugène Boudin.* Paris, 1899.

CAHEN, Gustave. *Eugène Boudin, sa vie, son œuvre.* Paris: H. Floury, 1900.

JEAN-AUBRY, Georges. *Eugène Boudin d'après des documents inédits. L'homme et l'œuvre.* Paris: Bernheim-Jeune, 1922. Neuchâtel: Ides et Calendes, 1968.

ROGER-MARX, Claude. *Eugène Boudin.* Paris: Crès, 1927.

CARIO, Louis. *Eugène Boudin.* Paris: Rieder, 1928.

BENJAMIN, L. Ruth. *Eugène Boudin.* New York: Raymond & Raymond, 1937.

CUNNINGHAM, Charles L. «Some Still-Lifes by Boudin,» in *Studies in the History of Art.* London: Phaidon for the Samuel Kress Foundation, 1959, pp. 382-392.

TEIXERA LEITE, Jose Roberto. *Boudin no Brasil.* Rio de Janeiro, 1961.

SCHMIT, Robert. *Eugène Boudin. Catalogue raisonné.* Paris: Robert Schmit, 3 vol., 1973.

KNYFF, Gilbert de. *Eugène Boudin raconté par lui-meme: sa vie, son atelier, son œuvre.* Paris: Mayer, 1976.

LIST OF ILLUSTRATIONS

We wish to thank the owners of the pictures reproduced herein, as well as those collectors who did not want to have their names mentioned. Our special thanks go to Mr. Charles Durand-Ruel and to the Galerie Schmit in Paris for their kind and valuable assistance:

MUSEUMS

FRANCE

Musée des Beaux-Arts, André Malraux, Le Havre.
Musée Eugène Boudin, Honfleur.
Louvre, Cabinet des Dessins, Paris.
Louvre, Musée du Jeu de Paume, Paris.
Musée Marmottan, Paris.

UNITED KINGDOM

Ashmoleum Museum, Oxford.

U.S.A.

The High Museum of Art, Atlanta, Georgia.
The Art Institute, Chicago.
The Metropolitan Museum of Art, New York.
National Gallery of Art, Washington D.C.

GALLERIES

Acquavella Galleries, New York – Marwan Hoss, Paris – Galerie Schmit, Paris.

PRIVATE COLLECTIONS

Mr. and Mrs. Paul Mellon, Upperville, Virginia – Mr. Walter, H. Annenberg, USA.

PHOTOGRAPHS

Photos Lécluse, Honfleur – Studio Lourmel 77, Paris – Photorama, Le Havre – Service de Documentation Photographique de la Réunion des Musées Nationaux, Paris – Otto E. Nelson, New York – Gene Trindl, Studio City, California.